CW00865294

YESTERDAY'S LUNCH

Learning to Digest the Past and
Develop a Hunger for Tomorrow's Dessert

KENNA WREN AILA

WESTBOW
PRESS®
A DIVISION OF THOMAS NELSON
& ZONDERVAN

Scripture quotations marked AMP are taken from the Amplified® Bible, Copyright © 2015 by The Lockman Foundation. Used by permission.

Scripture quotations marked KJV are taken from the King James Version of the Bible.

This book is a work of non-fiction. Unless otherwise noted, the author and the publisher make no explicit guarantees as to the accuracy of the information contained in this book and in some cases, names of people and places have been altered to protect their privacy.

WestBow Press books may be ordered through booksellers or by contacting:

WestBow Press
A Division of Thomas Nelson & Zondervan
1663 Liberty Drive
Bloomington, IN 47403
www.westbowpress.com
1 (866) 928-1240

ISBN: 978-1-9736-5229-8 (sc)
ISBN: 978-1-9736-5230-4 (hc)
ISBN: 978-1-9736-5228-1 (e)

Library of Congress Control Number: 2019901316

Print information available on the last page.

WestBow Press rev. date: 2/11/2019

MY AMBIVALENCE

I was two; you were strong. As I grew, another came along.

I was five; you were tall. Luckily, I can't remember it all.

I was seven; you were twelve. By then, rape was something I stored on the wall.

I said no, only twelve; my relief as my baby died hurt more than I can tell.

I was twelve; you were sixteen—once transpired into years.

You were a ghost, a monster, a promise to renege on.

You took me to where pain was real, but I was gone.

It hurt to sit, it hurt to walk; I never had the courage to run.

The fear of becoming two numbed by the fear of the extinguishing of one.

You were mean and violent, you were close and safe.

You couldn't hurt me, you never cared anyway.

I was fifteen; you were nineteen. She was pregnant; you were gone.

Then your void filled by another just as you had done.

So went by my eighteen years marred with pain and passed by rape.

Ghost after ghost seemed to steal my fate.

The muck left by scars too deep to cover; some skillfully carved by an absent other.

Always hungry, never seen, ever dirty, impossible to clean.

Don't see, or hear, or speak of the evil. I was to blame and not worth the upheaval.

"Feelings don't matter. Don't let those tears fall."

Emotions beaten out of me, I learned to cage the squall.

I told myself the innocence they took was a small thing.

The determination to survive then somehow offered wings.

Fly away I could, and often would—though never really leave.

My mind played tricks on me, and stunned, I'd happily agree.

Build the walls, make them strong; the work was intense but before long,

I couldn't see out, nor could any come in. I was surrounded. I'd let them win.

The process of digging back out I deplored, now pleading to find what I yearned to ignore.

A shroud of terror settled over with a hiss: "You'll never make it. Wasn't ignorance bliss?"

Like a screeching song, I swayed this way and that, afraid to uncover, trying desperately to go back.

There's no easy answer from the valley to the skies. It's uphill ahead, a steeper climb behind.

The past riddled with traps, spears aimed at my heart.

Healing in the skies ahead, terror waiting with a million darts.

But between what was and what could be loomed a bridge precarious to cross.

The message that was is already etched on the tablet of my heart.

When grief and pain have lived so long on the place I must next step.

That slippery slope where I hold on tight is also where I hold my next breath.

Memories behind, fears ahead; years covered with the lies I've heard, my face with the tears I've shed.

They'll come crashing down as I tread on that bridge enveloped in the anguish I bled.

And I'll know I was right to wait, standing there looking at a world devoured by hate.

The gorge is wide and the fall is deep, and never did I learn how to fly.

But now I realize the rainbow's end has become too bright to hide.

The bridge I see is my battered reflection hiding the safety that the rainbow is

Muting the colors and distorting the view; it's my reflection that casts a disorienting hue.

"Step across," I hear them say, but fear cries out angrily, "You know the price you'll pay!"

Walking over the past rewound is like hopping over land mines as my heart does pound.

My stomach knows better and tries to warn me, flipping and stomping and rolling inside me.

But still, they gently usher me along as if it were possible to change what's already been gone.

Still I look, and the rainbow is.

Red flows with love, the wasting of war.

Orange rushes over, saying goodbye to the lore.

Yellow screams its brightness, healing of scars once torn.

Green is reaching out, eyes opened beyond the storm.

Blue holds peace, no longer broken and worn.

Purple is the badge I've won. I'll make it and find it was worth the war.

I'll quiet the voices that say all is lost. I'll grow wings and use them—I'll learn how to soar.

A Future and a Hope

I am a survivor. But I'm not just a survivor; I'm also a wife and a mother. I'm a daughter, a sister, and an aunt. I love spending time with my husband and children. I teach children, and they're awesome company.

I love reading, playing the keyboard, listening to music, and gardening. I love spending time with the Lord. My life has been greatly enriched by the goodness of God—it's been redeemed in fact. The mercy of God is everlasting, and His faithfulness endures forever. My life is a testimony to God's grace, limitless forgiveness, and the miraculous beauty of His covenant in me.

I am a survivor because He is my Savior. I am able to endure because He endured more than I can ever know, and I can walk in joy because I was and am the joy set before Him. I am free from shame because He, despising the shame, sat on the right hand of the Father and is ever making intercession for me. He has promised a double portion for my shame, and He doesn't lie. I am alive because of His death, and He lives so I can die to sin; my life is hidden in Him. He is my forever, my strength, my song, my deliverer, my everlasting Father, my peace—and I am not forgotten.

I am a survivor of every type of abuse and neglect out there to one degree or another. I learned experientially that no matter what was going on around me, it could always be worse, and that kind of perspective is an incredible gift; it allowed me to look at the storm and think, *Behind those clouds, the sun is still in the sky, the stars will be out tonight, and the planet has not spun off its axis. God is my salvation, and His glory is my rear guard. I will not be afraid.* But that perspective came at a high price, and I lost it for many years.

When I was a little girl, hope was not a reality to me, nor was it something I missed. At age seven or eight, I had already decided that there was not, could not really be a God out there. My reality did not match the stories I heard in church of a loving God's miraculous power. I did not feel His love or see His provision, nor did I sense His peace and protection. The nightmares seemed more real to me; my reality was fear, loneliness, and despair.

One particular afternoon, it was storming in the house as much as it was outside. My siblings and I were home alone as usual, and my older siblings were at war. My older brother was trying to break into my older sister's bedroom, where she was hiding and rightly so—my brother had a butcher knife. Eventually, my brother simmered down some and went on a tirade in the backyard.

I followed him looking for an escape—some kind of way out. I saw the sun peeking through the clouds and remembered hearing someone say that when you see sunbeams, it's because someone died and went to heaven. But I knew better. Looking across the yard, I noticed an old, discarded tire from our family car that my brother had just sent sailing through the yard in anger. I remembered the Old Testament stories I had heard in church, and I timidly walked over to the tire and stepped in it. I was so angry, so tired. I remembered hearing the stories about Armageddon and the battles that would take place at the end of time, and I thought, *I'm too tired to fight.*

I looked up and said, "God, if you're really there, pick me up out of this tire and put me down somewhere else." Of course, nothing seemed to happen, but as I crumpled inside and began to step out of that tire, a quiet peace came over me and I was totally enveloped by the love of God. I immediately knew beyond all doubt that God was real. I could feel Him! I stepped out of that tire with a calm assurance that someday, everything would be all right.

Many years passed before my reality changed to match the promise I felt in my heart that day.

By the time I was in my early twenties, I had survived so much but overcome so little. My heart's cry was to no longer be someone else's story. I didn't want to be someone's victim. I was a wife; I had just given birth to my firstborn. I couldn't allow her to grow up in the chaos

I had endured growing up. I knew that in my present state, I couldn't be the mom she would need, and I so wanted to be that for her.

I declared to myself that I would no longer be the victim. I would learn to digest the past and develop a hunger for tomorrow's dessert. I spent the entire day studying my Bible to accomplish my goal. I went to bed feeling something very new—hope. *Now, things will be different.*

The next day, I woke up feeling no different than I had the morning before. I was frustrated and discouraged. Then I was asked a question: *Did you make one decision to follow Me?* I thought about the last several years of my life. *Is this a trick question?* I had rededicated myself to the Lord but had slipped back into those old habits so many times that it had become brassy even to me.

Over the years, though, my resolution had gained in strength as my faith in the Lord grew through the ministry of my pastor and others. *Yes, it takes just one decision*, I thought, not quite sure of my answer. I remembered all those times after I had rededicated my life to the Lord that I'd had opportunities to return to sin. *Every time you walked away from temptation, you committed more to trust your life to Me,* God said.

All those years growing up, I was waiting for something huge to happen in my life so that I could change once and for all and mark on my calendar that day as the day I went from a heathen to the world's strongest Christian. Many opportunities came up, but each time, I seemed to fail. Suddenly, I understood. One decision rebirthed my spirit from death to life, but there were a million tiny decisions that caused my corrupted flesh to lose ground and my spirit to be reborn; that caused a transformation on the outside that was as beautiful and profound as the one on the inside. This is the story of my journey.

CHAPTER 1

On the Outside

My name is Kenna Wren Aila, but everyone calls me Fire, which is what Kenna means. Actually, it means "born from fire." My sister was six when I was born. She had curly red hair, a million freckles, and the determination to harness a bear. I also had a brother three years older than me who had the smarts to trick the bear into harnessing itself. My baby sister was born two and a half years after me, and she had stringy, dirty-blond hair like mine. She was so pretty that with one smile, the bear would have willingly gone into any harness.

We lived in a small, yellow, stucco house on a hill in a quiet neighborhood just a few doors from my pastor's house. We spent as much time as we could outside; I remember the yard well. We had a brick path down to the street from our front door that we had helped to lay. On one side was the driveway, and on the other was the lawn with a locust tree in the middle. We loved to eat the beans from that tree!

All across the front of the house were rose bushes of different colors, and beyond those was a wooden fence shielding the shed from the street. On the other side of the house were two big cottonwood trees that housed our many tree houses with a playhouse in the middle that my grandfather had built before I was born. The backyard held many fruit trees, grape vines, and mint patches along with huge sunflowers all of which satisfied our hungry bellies on occasion.

My brother and I played safari in a large patch of tall weeds. We made machetes out of sticks and whacked our way through it undaunted by the danger we were sure awaited us inside. One day, my brother and I accidentally burned it all down.

Our house's three bedrooms became four when my parents converted the garage into a small bedroom for them and a bigger living room for the family with a huge, wood-burning Franklin stove. The layout of the house changed often because my parents enjoyed remodeling. My mom moved walls the way most women change their decor. She also moved the plumbing, electrical, and anything else that felt out of place to her. She still hasn't found the right place for everything!

She loved to sew; that was made obvious by all the fabric and thread she collected for the projects she planned to do someday. She also worked in child care, and she retired as a toymaker with my dad.

My dad worked in television until he was injured and could no longer work. Before that, though, he left for work at the same time every morning and came home at the same time every night. He fixed the family cars and taught us how to fix our bikes, and he made us laugh. He loved to watch Charlie Chaplain, the Three Stooges, Red Skelton, and Abbott and Costello, and he taught us to love them too. He worked out of town a lot when we were small, and I always missed him terribly when he was gone.

My parents were heavily involved in our church. My dad led the praise and worship and played his guitar, and my mom sang backup and sometimes played her violin. They taught children's church and sometimes led the youth, and they sponsored VBS and attended summer camps with the church kids. We were a busy family.

I attended kindergarten through fourth grade in our neighborhood elementary school. I was in choir and orchestra, both of which I enjoyed though I never did master a stringed instrument.

When I was almost ten, my parents bought a house in the more affluent part of town, and I began fifth grade at a new school with new rules and strange dynamics. I went to another new school for sixth and most of seventh grade.

Our new house had white siding with green trim and redbrick accents. It was on top of a hill with a deck in the backyard. Later, my parents bought a huge pond that we all helped put in. The view was amazing especially at night when all the city lights were sparkling and the stars were twinkling. We slept out on that deck many nights.

Our yard was split up into three tiers, and the bottom tier was our self-claimed play space. My brother and I dug a fort into the ground that was six feet deep, six feet long, and four feet wide. We put a full sheet of plywood over it and then hid it under a thin layer of dirt. We dug a tunnel to our fort and made a trapdoor with an old, dried-up Christmas tree tied to a smaller sheet of plywood. Our fort was complete. We stocked it with water and crackers and had a blast in our cool, dark hiding place. Eventually, my dad took an unfortunate spill into our fort when the board broke as he was walking through the yard. He was furious! He ranted and raved about how we could have been killed. Luckily, he never found the one we had dug beside it.

Wherever we lived, there were times when our home was filled with laughter. My parents didn't just allow but encouraged a playful attitude during the seasons in our lives. They threw parties on the deck beside the pond with Hawaiian kabobs and twirly umbrellas, and they invited all our friends. Inevitably, a water fight ensued; the whole mob of us ran through the house with buckets of water and anything else we could find in the war of the century. My friends didn't mind hanging out at my house because my parents were so laid back.

My parents worked a lot of hours, and they loved to go out for pie and coffee or donuts. And yard sales were always calling out to them. My older sister watched us as best she could, but she was young too. Overall, we were fairly loosely supervised. Sometimes, I joke that we were raised by the coyotes in the mesa near our home. We carried many of the responsibilities of our home at an amazingly early age. By the time I was five, I knew how to make my own eggs and hot cereal and had tried many recipes in experimental baking—totally inedible of course.

When I began second grade, I was excited as I walked into my bedroom and it was clean! There were clothes hanging in the closet and even folded in my dresser drawers. I was ecstatic! I remember running to the closet with joy and trying on all my fresh, clean dresses. Unfortunately, I didn't bother to hang them up. My mother told me that she was tired of my clean clothes going to the floor, so from then on, if I wanted clean laundry, I had to wash it myself.

My brother and I loved to play on the mountain of clothes that inhabited the laundry room, and I will never forget the small pinkies we found one day. I thought they were so cute, but my brother knew their nuisance and shot them with his BB gun the following day.

My siblings and I had chores from as early as I can remember. Too young to reach the sink, I stood on a stool to do dishes, the water running down my sleeves and into my shirt. By the time I was ten, dinner was solely my responsibility at least once a week, and I had to clean the entire kitchen one week out of every month. My parents struggled with consistently ensuring that we kept up, so we cleaned sometimes and cooked sometimes. Even with all our responsibilities, it seems we had an unreal amount of free time on our hands.

CHAPTER 2

On the Inside

My room was the last door on the right down a short
hallway; I shared it with my younger and older sisters until
after the remodeling, when my older sister got a room of
her own. It was a house similar to many others around it
I'm sure. Through the front door was the living room, and
past that was the kitchen. To the right of the living room
ran the hallway to our bathroom and bedrooms, and to the
left was my parents' small room. Past the kitchen was the
laundry room.

Our house was usually dirty and cluttered. My bedroom
floor was rarely visible under all the junk, laundry, and trash
that littered the floor. One night when I was very young,
my parents were gone and my older sister was putting

my baby sister and me to bed. I remember the amazing feeling of those clean, crisp sheets falling over me as my sister remade the bed with freshly washed linens. I was so excited, and the sheets smelled so nice. I don't know how often that may have happened; it was rare that we even had sheets on our beds.

From the outside, our house was pretty and the yard was fairly well maintained. That mirrored how our family was perceived. Nobody really knew the horror we lived in every day. We looked good on the outside, but I was miserable on the inside. There are a lot of things I just don't remember or remember only bits and pieces of. I remember spoiled, moldy food and maggots in the fridge, mice in the laundry room, and grass growing on my bedroom floor. Groceries were brought into the house about every month or so, but they usually came from discount stores where their remaining shelf life was bleak at most. That led to a multitude of spoiled food and not much else.

I knew at an early age that we didn't have enough money; I felt that we just didn't have money at all. Packing my lunch in elementary school was an embarrassing chore.

I packed white bread all squished down with margarine, cinnamon, and sugar on it because that was all I could find. I hid it in my hands as I ate so no one could see what I was eating. One time, I had a school assignment to write everything down that I had eaten for three days. My mother saw it and made me change what it said.

The emotional climate of our home was ever changing as the tide of my mother's emotional disposition tossed it, and with it, we hung on tightly as those waves tossed us to and fro. We never knew which side of her we'd face. Sometimes, she did some really cool stuff with us like screen printing or making homemade jelly and donuts. Then the next thing we knew, she was stomping around, screaming, and yelling about what we were not sure. We didn't know how to make her stop, but we were all sure we had caused it.

She yelled a lot, and the whole house seemed to spin on her every whim. If she didn't see things happen the way she thought they should have, she would huff around, slam doors, and half-throw everything she had in her hands, calling us all by our full names. We'd come running and hoping we hadn't kindled her wrath too much.

She had an amazingly horrible talent for making me feel everything was my fault. I endured spankings and unimaginable fear every time I did anything wrong. Our paddle was yellow with a red stripe painted all around the edges like racing stripes. It was maybe twelve inches long and about an inch thick with half-inch holes drilled through it. We were to stand with our palms against the wall while that thing flew over and over.

Once during a paddling, my mother asked if I was done screaming yet. I couldn't understand what that meant as I was getting a beating at the time. Once I got up the courage to ask what she meant, she said that as long as I was screaming, she knew she hadn't broken "it" yet. She didn't stop until we quit crying or were at least whimpering moderately. Several times, I made the mistake of putting my hands across my rear. When I got back to my bedroom, my fingers were raw.

Then the tide would change; we'd get away with everything, and she would laugh all through it. Those moods didn't last long, however; we'd turn around and she would be yelling and crying again, slamming doors and whatever else she had in her hands, and we all scrambled for something to clean as she screamed about the filth in the house. We knew that if we could get it clean, she'd eventually calm down. Usually when she saw we were cleaning up the place, she would leave the house in a rage. We cleaned as quickly as we could terrified of what would happen if she came back and we weren't done. When she did return, the ranting and raving would always resume, that time about how we had driven her to rage because it was the only way she could get the house clean.

Most of my memories are not pleasant, but some are. I remember going camping, taking long drives along scenic routes, and eating ice cream with pretzels while watching movies. Most of what I remember was their not being home. I spent my childhood days in constant fear. My earliest memory is of me lying on the bathroom floor of our little house while the older boys from next door explored what should have been my most secret part with their fingers and whatever else was lying around. I was potty-training, maybe two years old. Every time I was in the bathroom, they were there too supposedly helping me. Many times, I was just walking through the house and all of the sudden I would feel the most intense pain I assume now from all that was going on. I fell to the floor screaming in a fetal position waiting for the pain to subside. My mom and siblings would ask each other what was wrong but then just shrug. I wasn't about to tell them.

One time, I did tell my mom. Those same boys had taken turns exploring me with a 16-penny nail. I told my mom calmly as if I were describing the weather. I was shocked when she totally flipped out. She cried for days and kept asking if I was sure it wasn't just a fingernail—as if that would have been better. She took me to the doctor, and I experienced my first pelvic exam on a changing table at age three. I have no idea what the doctor reported, but I decided I'd be much better off if I kept my mouth shut. And I did for a very long time.

I attended my first slumber party when I was five. My older sister had a friend several blocks from our house who was having a birthday party, so I tagged along. Most of the party I have forgotten, but I do remember three slots of time. It was the first time I was raped. A woman came in and yelled at a man, but I don't know what happened next.

In the morning as we were getting ready to leave, the man asked me how old I was, and I remember telling him I was five. The man smiled and nodded at me as if in approval of something. When the woman dropped us off at home, she told my mother that she had caught the man on top of me the night before. My mother replied, "Oh, I'm sure she's fine," as she tousled my hair. No one ever mentioned it again, so I figured I was indeed fine.

When my baby sister was four, she and I were playing outside with my older brother in our backyard with the neighbor boys across the fence. One of the boys threw a piece of floor tile and hit my baby sister. My parents rushed her to the hospital; her wound required stitches. After that, those boys weren't allowed around much, and that chapter of my nightmare came to an end.

Nights were very scary times for me. I had crazy, recurring dreams that seemed so real. In one of those dreams, I was riding a tricycle as fast as I could. I was terrified as I looked over my shoulder at a crazy man in the truck driving after me and hanging out the window laughing with a sickly grin.

Another dream I had a lot starred the same crazed man in it, but I couldn't see him until the end of the dream when he would pop out of a box and smile the same sick smile before I'd startle awake again in terrified agony.

One morning as the rest of the house bustled around getting ready for the day, I lay frozen in my bed convinced a group of men with guns had gathered on the street in front of my house. I was scared to get off the top bunk because I'd have to cross in front of my bedroom window, and I knew they'd be able to see me. I tried to warn the rest of the house. I was confused as to why they couldn't see the men and weren't afraid. Eventually, I peeked out and saw no one there; I realized it must have been a dream.

I never liked using public bathrooms as a child; I'd beg to be allowed to wait until we got home. I'd have tears in my eyes and my heart would race as the room began to spin. It would have meant many hours as we wandered whatever store my mother had found herself in, usually a cloth or hobby store. Threatened with spanking, a threat that was made good many times, I spun into what I now know was a panic attack as I hesitantly heard the door close behind me. Every time I heard an exhaust fan, I felt as though I was at death's door, and an overwhelming urge to run took over me though I had learned to freeze instead. I looked all around expecting the scary man from my dreams to pop out at any moment to get me again. The sound of the toilet flushing was as terrifying as the visions in my head, and I tore out of those bathrooms as if something vicious were at my heels. I was sure something was.

School was a wonderful and scary place at the same time. The bathrooms were huge in my little eyes and seemed to be a dungeon of unknown fears a million miles from my classroom. Using the bathrooms at school was no different; I was terrified to do so. The only place I felt safe was next to my teacher, and of course I wasn't permitted to stay there much.

All through my elementary years, I struggled socially and academically. I easily understood the material, but I couldn't stay organized or focused enough to complete and turn in assignments. I was always on guard, and as a result, I missed a lot of instruction as my mind wandered every time I heard a word that triggered another memory or thought.

Many times, I felt disconnected to what was going on around me. Sometimes, I'd have a strange, tingly feeling and then everything around me would appear to be shifting as if the walls were moving and things were moving about on them in a war. When I was little, those episodes got me in trouble because I'd lose track of what was actually going on around me.

One time when I was in first or second grade, I was at school writing a story. I became so enthralled in the story that I sort of went there. When I snapped out of it, my teacher was glaring at me; I was in a lot of trouble. Apparently, I had been vocalizing loudly what my character was experiencing.

Another time, my mom was driving us to pick up my dad from work. I was riding in the front seat, and my older sister was in the back seat directly behind me. I don't really know what happened, but in my head, we were parked at my dad's work and it was time to get out of the car to pick him up. I unlocked and opened my door to climb out. That was when I saw the asphalt zooming by underneath us and realized we were still driving down the freeway. My older sister grabbed my door from behind and pulled it closed. I wasn't allowed to sit in the front seat for quite a while.

When I was a child, there was one place where I never felt afraid, and that was at my pastor's house. He and his family lived a few doors down from us on the far end of the street. I used to walk down the road to their house and ask if their oldest daughter could play. She was in high school, but they always let me in and were so kind. And they always fed me. I was in second or third grade when they stepped down. I sat at my bedroom window and looked down the street wishing I could be there again.

A new pastor moved into the parsonage with one son whom they had adopted; he was several years older than me. I was in the second grade when it all started again, much of which I don't remember. I do remember the nightmares, pain, and confusion as everyone else went about life. His family pastored the church we attended. I was very young and had very limited understanding of sexual relationships or human reproductive systems, so I spent years afraid that

I was pregnant or had AIDS. Our home was dirty, and our nutritional support was meager, so I was sick all the time, and when my third-grade teacher did a unit on AIDS, I was sure she was staring right at me and knew everything.

I went to a neighbor's house in the middle of the day during that year and saw a woman breaking up with her boyfriend on a soap opera. I imagined myself telling the boy the same thing, but I was too afraid. When he began raping me, I was already so conditioned to the abuse that it didn't seem significant to me.

Once, my brother caught him after he'd lured me under the bed in my room and had taken my panties down, telling me he was only going to "do it for a minute." When my mom asked me about it, I was afraid I'd get in trouble, so I told her that I had been getting dressed when he walked into the room and that I ducked under the bed; that was why my panties were down around my ankles. She was quick to believe me.

I was in fourth grade the first time he told me, "I hope you don't get pregnant." There I was alone and wondering what happened to girls who got pregnant. I didn't have enough knowledge to know that wasn't yet possible for me, but I cannot describe the fear and dread I felt that moment. It was as if my life were already over. The realization of what had been going on rushed over me like a deadly tidal wave. I felt I was going to drown in it; I kind of wished I could have. Later that day, I walked in circles in our well shed thinking I was going to have to marry that boy if I didn't want to burn in hell.

I had many nightmares of myself standing in front of the judgment seat of God surrounded by everyone I knew—my family especially. God was on His throne in front of me as I stood alone looking at Him. He was asking me why I had let this happen knowing it was wrong. My mom was glaring at me, and all the others just shook their heads at me in shame.

Another dream that haunted me took place at school. He was chasing me through my fourth-grade classroom and I was begging him, "Not here!" I was in tears, and I knew that everyone would know. I woke up crying many times hoping for it all to end. It didn't end until a week before my tenth birthday, when we moved to the other side of town.

The years had already taken their toll, and the more I thought about the shame of others finding out, the harder I worked to cover it up. I'm not sure if things actually got worse when we moved across town or if they just seemed worse because I was older and more aware. My parents were gone even more. I lived across the street from the elementary school where I attended fifth grade. It was my responsibility most days to get my baby sister and myself to school. I didn't usually remember to bathe or brush my hair or teeth. There wasn't usually much to eat either.

One warm afternoon, we had gone outside while my parents were gone, which was strictly forbidden but a rule we never followed. We were riding our bikes in the front yard with the neighbor kids. Their grandma came outside and brought them lunch, instructed them to sit down and eat, and stood there to make sure they did. I remember thinking how strange that was and how yummy their food smelled.

I somehow got through the year though my grades and social life were not spectacular. I knew the school staff was concerned. My teacher took me aside several times to ask me if there was anything going on at home that she should be concerned about. I assured her that everything was fine, that I just missed my mom because she had to work a lot. Several days later, I saw my mom on school campus with the counselor, but to my knowledge, nothing ever happened as a result of that.

One morning as I was getting ready for school, my mom was sewing something and called for my baby sister and me. We went to her, and she burst into tears and told us how awful we looked. My heart sank; I had worked all morning to find something nice to wear and had chosen a gray sweatshirt and a purple skirt my older sister had made for me out of a discarded pair of her jeans. I walked away bewildered and not sure what to do.

Many afternoons, my baby sister and I came home to an empty house locked up tight. We got tired of the struggle to finagle our way in and walked to a friend's house. We explained that there wasn't anyone home and asked if we could stay there for a while. I guess they called my mom, and she told them that we were lying, that there was a key in the backyard. The woman looked at me angrily, and I shrank in embarrassment. After that, we'd go home and climb under the deck in the backyard until someone came home.

Sixth grade started, and my school changed, but my awkwardness and horrific hygiene stayed the same. My clothes were always dirty, and I was scared to shower; I always felt that some unseen horror was lurking close by. When I was little, the rule was that we had to take a bath every Sunday morning before church. I didn't have any further instruction on the matter, so I still followed the same expectation mostly. Sometimes I missed, and weeks would go by without my taking a shower.

I was embarrassed to eat with others because I saw the filth on my hands as I reached for food. My teachers had several "interventions" during which they spoke to the class as a whole about hygiene. It didn't register that they were actually talking to me.

I wore the same pair of pants every day because my other pair had gotten ripped. One day, a girl stopped me in the hall and talked to me about taking baths, wearing clean clothes, and brushing my hair and teeth. I was so ashamed that I took a three-hour bath that afternoon. I had not been aware of my lack of hygiene before that.

I became a bit compulsive about taking baths and wearing clean clothes, and I began cleaning the house more. The kitchen counters were usually stacked to the upper cabinets with trash, discarded food, and dirty dishes, and the other living spaces were equally full of trash and debris most of the time. We had dogs in the house, and that only added to the nastiness. The environment didn't lend itself to doing homework, and nobody was there to check if I even had any homework. At the end of my sixth grade, my GPA in language was 15 percent.

One day during sixth grade, I felt especially lonely and angry. I wanted out of my house so badly. I made a plan to run away. I packed a grocery sack with a few canned goods and a couple of shirts, and I got a block away from my house before I realized that no one would notice my absence. I thought about the section of ditch I had planned to live in close to my school so I could still attend it. I realized that no matter where I went, I would follow myself, and my problems would come too. I thought about the kids from school who would be walking by on their way home in the afternoons and how they would make fun of me for being there. Not wanting the attention that would bring, I decided to go home. When I arrived, my brother saw the bag and glared at me. I didn't try that one again.

We found a new church when we moved, and I eventually made some friends there. I started drinking and smoking, and by the time I was twelve, I was smoking two or three packs some days, mostly stolen cigarettes. I had taken my first drag of a cigarette when I was five behind the cherry tree in my backyard with my brother and one of the boys who was molesting me.

When I was ten or eleven, I rode my bike around the neighborhood to find discarded cigarette butts to suck on for the momentary release that short buzz afforded me. Once after coming back home, I was in the bathroom washing the cigarette smell off my hands, when my dad walked by and asked, "Putting another nail in your coffin?" He just walked away.

I stole packs of cigarettes from the store or bought them from the coin machines in the back of restaurants. In seventh grade, I spent my lunches in the school bathroom smoking and vandalizing school property. Near the end of the year, I was caught smoking behind some trees near the field of my middle school. The principal found a whole pack of cigarettes in my jacket pocket. They called my mom and planned to suspend me for a week. I told my mom that the cigarettes weren't mine. She went to the school and explained that it was her fault because she had always taught us to respect authority; that was why I hadn't argued with the principal when I was caught. She took me out of the school, and I was never allowed to go to school again despite my begging and pleading.

When I was twelve, a new family including a seventeen-year-old son and a fourteen-year-old daughter started attending our new church. He gave me lots of attention, wrote me a letter sprayed with his cologne, and complimented me often. I was nervous, excited, and confused all at the same time. This guy was really cute, and I couldn't believe he was interested in me. His little sister and I began hanging out, going to the movies and shopping at the mall, and I spent the night at her house several times. The first time he climbed onto me, I told him it hurt and pushed him off. He listened to me; his sister was sleeping just feet away.

He came to my house too. My parents were sponsoring a youth group out of our home at the time, and we met every week. He and I sat around the house and yard, kissing, hugging, and holding hands. We were affectionate at the church too. I was only twelve; I cannot imagine how that was allowed to go on.

One night, his sister invited me to a movie. My brother's best friend dropped me off, and no one was home but he and his four-year-old brother. That was the first night that he raped me. I told him no several times, but I really didn't fight him physically. His little brother was outside the bedroom banging on the door the whole time. When it was over, I just got dressed and went on as if nothing had happened.

Two weeks after the first rape, it happened again. That time, there were lots of people at his house. I guess we were having a party or something, but I can't remember the rest of the night very clearly. He asked me if I wanted to go to the garage to check out his new stereo speakers. He raped me again. There were no contraceptives involved, and two weeks after my period was supposed to have started, I stole a pregnancy test from the store. It came out positive.

I eventually got up the courage to tell my brother what had happened, and he marched me into my parents' bedroom and told them I had something to say and then left me to face them alone. I don't think I have ever felt more alone, scared, or betrayed than at that moment. I told them what had happened and then stood there as they discussed their options. My mom made a doctor's appointment, and the day before we were supposed to go, I was so relieved when I thought my period had come.

After my second pelvic exam, the doctor wrote it up as a spontaneous miscarriage. I had turned thirteen, and my mom and baby sister sat at my feet the entire time. That was almost more violating than the rape.

The detectives came to the doctor's office to take my statement and explain what would happen next. I would go to the courthouse, and they would record my deposition. Scared, I agreed.

A few days later, my mom told me that my youth pastor at the time had explained to her what date rape was—it meant I had been asking for it but had changed my mind at the last minute. She told me that if I was lying, the boy could get in a lot of trouble. I just nodded and walked away. I hurt so badly and was so numb all at the same time.

At the next appointment, I asked the detectives what would happen to the boy if he was found guilty. The woman answered, "Oh, he'll just have to take some classes." *That's it?* I wondered. I told them I no longer wanted to press charges. Later, my mom asked me if I had ever had sex with anyone besides him. *She still doesn't believe me*, I thought. I shook my head and lied. "No."

My older siblings were in high school then or should have been, and they had begun drinking, smoking, doing drugs, and sneaking out. For me, getting involved in such behavior was a natural progression though drugs were never an option for me; my older siblings took care of that. They told me what would happen if they ever caught me doing drugs, and I had no trouble believing them. I suddenly felt some control over what was happening in my life.

As I got older, I became more comfortable and less terrified by those strange experiences of feeling disconnected with what was going on around me—the strange, tingly feeling in my body and then everything around me shifting, again the walls moving and things moving about on them. They became almost calming, like watching waves on the ocean or wind blowing the trees. I learned to experience it like an escape from the horror I was in.

My teenage years were a myriad of chaos and lies, as the putrescence I tried so hard to ignore began to drain out like pus from an infection. The faster it drained, the harder I ran to escape the stench. My reflection was wasted, tired, and corrupt. My actions matched how I felt, and the hole I was in kept getting deeper.

My older sister married her own version of a nightmare and moved away. I got to visit her for a while until she and my mother fell out. Then I would sneak out to see my sister. She always greeted me as if I were the most important person in her life. I loved that about her. After her own bout with drugs, she and my brother sternly warned me that if I ever got caught with them, I'd be sorry. I'm still so thankful to them for that—one less train wreck I'd inevitably have to clean up.

My parents had a habit of constantly taking in strays to live in our house. At age twelve, I became the full-time nanny for a woman's five-month-old and fifteen-month-old. I cared for them day and night; I did their laundry, cooked their food (what little I could scratch up), gave them baths, and supervised them in between. Then a neighbor needed care for his nineteen-month-old and two-year-old—again, twelve-hour days for me.

I wished I hadn't blown my chances to go to school. I had nightmares about being an adult trying to maneuver through the halls of middle school. Always late, never tidy, missing homework and whole weeks of instruction because I was working and had forgotten to go to school. I would wake up in a cold sweat unsure of the reality of my waking hours.

Another stray was an older teenage boy who slept over often and lived with us off and on. I told myself that the relationship was perfect—no expectations, no one even knew. It wasn't rape if I never said no. For years, I didn't.

I was afraid of getting pregnant but more afraid of the continuance of my younger years.

The years went by in a blur, trauma on top of trauma. I was that corrupt kid at church and the invisible kid at home. I worked as much as I could, a welcome escape from the nightmare of my life. I earned money and begged to go back to school. I promised to pay the tuition for the small private school I had found, but the answer was still no. I yelled and told my mother I would have no future and would work in daycare all my life. I thought she was going to kill me right in my own house.

I never mentioned school again. I worked during the day and did everything I could think of to quiet the awareness of the tragedy my life had become. I sat around scratching at my wrists trying to make tangible some of the pain I felt. I drank, smoked, stole, and lied. I ate very little and struggled to keep it down when I did.

I wrote a lot and read more, anything to escape myself for a while. Most of the writing I did was like poetry, which was very calming. Walking through a park one day, I heard the leaves rustling through the trees. I was about fifteen, and I wondered what kind of legacy I would leave. The sound of the wind through the leaves was so calming. I thought about what kind of aura I carried around, what I left people after they'd been with me. I didn't have an answer, but I knew it mattered—I knew I wanted it to matter. I wanted my life to matter. I wanted to have an answer for people who demanded an explanation for why I still believed there was a God despite the circumstances I'd endured as a child. I didn't have an answer for that either, but I just knew. I didn't have the faith to call out to God, but I knew He was out there somewhere, that He loved me, and that my life wasn't His best for me.

When I was seventeen, I met a boy who was in the military. We became instantly inseparable unless he was at work. He bought me a pager so he could always get hold of me, and things got way too serious way too fast; I was always afraid of getting pregnant but more afraid of saying no to him.

After that, things went from bad to much, much worse. He didn't allow me to go out with my friends alone; he chose my clothes and where I went. He lived in an apartment on base, and once we were there, I was on his clock. He refused to take me home until I performed exactly as he wanted me to. He told me that if I tried to run, I'd be arrested because it was illegal for me to be on base. I totally gave up—I stopped trying. I submitted to his every whim. I had no fight left in me. We got engaged and flew out of state to meet his parents. I was eighteen, but I felt closer to eighty and ready for my long, tiring life to end.

My childhood pastors had returned to the church we had attended as children, and we had resumed attendance there also. One Sunday morning, I was in church when the music team began a new song; it talked about the redeeming blood of Jesus and the boldness it provided to enter the safety of His presence. I wondered if that were possible. That afternoon, I begged my fiancé to rededicate His life to the Lord with me. He refused, and somehow, I finally walked away from him. He followed me for a time, called me at work, and showed up everywhere I went, but eventually, the stalking stopped.

CHAPTER 3

Hope for What I'd Lost

As I entered adulthood, my view of the world was cynical and bleak. I had given up on any chance of a happy life much earlier, and I was searching for a chance to merely survive. The Lord blessed me with a good job at which I met the man I eventually married.

The year of our engagement was tough; I tried to declare my independence, and my mother held onto me tightly. In the end, I finally conceded to getting married and quit trying to attach my preferences to the ceremony. My mother and I had some of our worst fights that year ending in her fits of rage and my withdrawal.

Finally the day came, and as I stood in front of all those people, I felt as if I were in a dream—so disconnected. It all seemed so surreal; it was supposed to be the happiest day of my life, but I didn't feel much at all.

My husband endured so much during our first few years together as I tried desperately to connect with him while maintaining the disconnect from the pain I had lived in for so long. One minute we'd be laughing and wrestling around in play, and the next thing I knew, I was screaming in terror, punching him, and trying desperately to get free. He stared at me in confusion, stunned. I shrank back in shame, not sure of what had happened either. Sometimes, I was able to be intimate, but at other times, I burst into tears. Many times, I silently prayed for the Lord to help me to be the wife I felt he deserved.

We had two children over the next several years. The pregnancies were tough because I didn't have an ounce of faith in my ability to be a mother. As I slipped deeper into the depression I had battled for years, I feared what kind of life my children would have to endure. I continued to be plagued by nightmares and panic attacks; I had difficulty completing the most common tasks. Participating in a conversation was as daunting as anything else I faced; my attention constantly veered off in a different direction. I began to lose time; I wasn't sure what happened between the start and the end of many tasks. I felt more and more uncomfortable in my own skin and far less comfortable with being in the same room with anybody. As hard as I tried to bury my past, my present was getting buried along with it.

By that time in my life, I was so numb. It had literally been years since I had laughed, cried, or really felt much of anything but shame. I had no sense of direction or belonging; I was just very, very tired. It seemed as though I had already experienced as much life as I could handle.

Beauty *for* ashes! It was such an amazing realization when I heard it through my spirit as I read it. The same passages of scripture have so much layered meaning to them, and this layer completely astounded me. It changed my thinking forever. I learned a worship song when I was about ten—Isaiah 61:3 put to song. I had it stuck in my head for weeks as I struggled with who I could possibly be and to a child no less until I finally looked it up. I was so overwhelmed by what it said.

> The Spirit of the Lord God is upon me,
> Because the Lord has anointed and
>   commissioned me
> To bring good news to the humble and
>   afflicted;
> He has sent me to bind up [the wounds of]
>   the brokenhearted,
> To proclaim release [from confinement
>   and condemnation] to the [physical
>   and spiritual] captives And freedom to
>   prisoners, To proclaim [a]the favorable
>   year of the Lord, And the day of
>   vengeance and retribution of our God,
> To comfort all who mourn,
> To grant to those who mourn in Zion the
>   following:
> To give them a [c]turban instead of dust [on
>   their heads, a sign of mourning],
> The oil of joy instead of mourning,

The garment [expressive] of praise instead of
a disheartened spirit.

So they will be called the trees of
righteousness [strong and magnificent,
distinguished for integrity, justice, and
right standing with God],

The planting of the Lord, that He may be
glorified. (Isaiah 61:1–3 AMP)

As I read it, I saw in my mind's eye a market with a
basket of apples. It had a sign that read "Three for $1." I saw
myself buying the apples and handing the dollar over the
counter. Then I had a funny thought—*If I ran out of the store
with the apples and my dollar, would the apples really be mine?*
No, they wouldn't. God used this crazy scenario to show
me that I couldn't accept the beauty, joy, or the life of praise
to Him without giving up some stuff first—the ashes, the
sadness, the heaviness, and the depression that weighed on
my shoulders. I read it as a transaction—beauty *for* ashes.
I realized that I could have the oil of joy for mourning or
the garment of praise for the spirit of heaviness—I couldn't
walk away with both.

Over the next fifteen years, I grew in my church to an understanding of Jesus's unconditional love for me and how He had a plan for my life despite the challenges of my childhood. I found some hope in that. But every day was still a struggle to trust God with my heart. I prayed for a tender heart, but as my guards came down, everything hurt and I'd hurl them right back up.

I learned how to pray, and I worked in children and youth ministry and music ministry, and I even scrubbed toilets and handled anything else that needed to be done. The one hole I couldn't fill and didn't know how to trust God to fill was the feeling of being worthy because first, I had to learn to trust others. *My heart is damaged goods*, I thought. *Why would anyone work to preserve it?* I knew all the scriptures and could recite them and minister through them to others, but somewhere deep down, I couldn't believe they were true for me. I thought about how David loved God, worshipped Him, and set a place for His presence, the ark of the covenant. He committed to worshipping the Lord night and day to honor Him, but he made some pretty serious blunders too such having another man killed so he could have his wife. At the end of David's story, He was not allowed to build the temple for the Lord because he had too much blood on his hands. I took on that personification and completely discounted the New Testament grace that is available to us all. I knew I could clean toilets, but anything besides that seemed like more than I should be entrusted with.

During that time, I worked with kids from preschool to the teen years. I taught in a preschool, worked in a residential home for at-risk youth, and even cared for emotionally and behaviorally disturbed children through a foster care agency. What I learned about myself in those programs shined an uncomfortable light on my struggles, and though I was being fulfilled by my work more and more, I lost my ability to participate in my own life. I needed help desperately, but I had no idea how or where to find it.

Many times, I found myself looking for some kind of online therapy kit so I could feel some support without the shame and vulnerability I knew would follow. After an awkward anniversary celebration one year, I sat on the bed of our hotel room and googled "Christian therapy" in the town where we lived. A place popped up, and I looked through the faces of the professionals. My heart raced. My stomach flipped. I asked my husband what he thought about my trying it out. He supported the idea, and I played with my phone a little bit longer and then changed the subject. He brought it up again and again until finally, I called. I still wasn't even sure I needed therapy, but I made the appointment anyway.

I cried through the entire first session but didn't understand why. It took many months for me to really come to the point that I was ready to admit what a mess I was and relinquish some control. Reanimating the skeletons I'd worked so hard to bury was terrifying. The panic attacks, dissociative tendencies, irritability, and helplessness weighed so heavily on me that I didn't have the strength to move. All the physiological symptoms that had finally brought me to find some help exploded, but I still held on as tight as I could to the illusion that I had life conquered, that all I needed was a little adjusting to learn some skills in making my body cooperate when I told it to calm down.

But as I began the healing process, things seemed to get so much worse. As I learned how many of my daily habits were so maladjusted, I sometimes felt I'd implode with the stress. And some days, the reality of it all hit and I wasn't sure I'd be able to go on. The ugliness of my life caused such a feeling of being tainted and having nothing left to give. Visions of death began to flash before my eyes, and though the visions scared me, I also thought maybe that would be better. I thought, *My husband and children don't deserve to have to deal with the hot mess that I am.* I thought about the pretty, sweet, all-put-together wife my husband could find—after being tricked into marrying my craziness—and what a mother my children could have, someone who didn't carry the things I did that made me feel so incomplete.

Little by little, however, things began to brighten as I learned to trust my therapist and use the skills she was teaching me. It was a long, challenging journey with victories and failures as I learned a whole new way of maneuvering though my days. I felt a connection to my life that at first was so very unwelcome, but it turned into a joy to have relationship as I learned to trust the people around me more and more. The support they offered was a lifeline so many times when they didn't even know that's what it was.

After almost two years, I stopped therapy having been blessed with a wonderful, godly therapist. I was beginning to meet myself maybe for the first time ever. I was diagnosed with PTSD and bipolar II, meaning that mostly, my chemistry tended toward depression with a few rapid cycles of mania.

Medication eased the ups and downs and helped me feel safe, connected, and able to handle life and build meaningful relationships. The skills I learned in therapy taught me that trust was possible, that boundaries were healthy—even godly—and that my life wasn't over. I realized I was beginning a new season I never imagined could have happened for me. I was able to engage in a great job with a wonderful support system of friends whom I will always know I can count on, and I'm learning to trust more and more each day. I've experienced so much change in those two years professionally, personally, and spiritually. God taught me at every corner that He was still beside me.

One of my favorite Bible stories is that of Jonah. His life was in the will of God when the story starts as I imagine mine was even before I was born. He was a prophet whom God used to communicate with His people. God commissioned Jonah to go minister to the people of Nineveh. Jonah knew how sinful and violent they were, so he got in a boat headed the other direction. He was scared. I imagine he thought God was crazy for asking him to risk his life to save those people.

When Jonah stepped out in disobedience, a terrible storm came upon them, and Jonah admitted it was because of his disobedience that the storm had come. The men tried to save the ship afraid of hurting the man of God, but it became clear that it was their only option. So he was thrown into the sea to die.

God, however, didn't leave Jonah to die in the bed he had made for himself. The Bible says, "Now the Lord had prepared (appointed, destined) a great fish to swallow Jonah. And Jonah was in the stomach of the fish three days and three nights" (Jonah 1:17 AMP).

I imagine Jonah asked himself if his day could get any worse. First, he had been asked to evangelize a people who were evil through and through, and then his master plan to run failed when the storm came and he was thrown into the raging sea and then swallowed by a fish—what a way to go!

What Jonah didn't understand was that the fish was the mercy of God. Had the fish not come, Jonah would have received the judgment ordinary under the Old Covenant—death. But the Bible says that God had predestined and ordained that fish to swallow Jonah. It still took Jonah three days to repent and agree to go to Nineveh, and even in his obedience, he still hadn't submitted himself to the will of God as we see at the end of the story. Jonah watched from afar for the people to get exactly what he had predicted, to stay in the mire he had found them in, and for God to blow them up. But the people did repent, and the people of Nineveh turned their hearts to God.

My life did not go the way it was supposed to when I was growing up. I should have been protected, nurtured, tucked in at night, and awakened in the morning. I should have had meals and an education, and I should have been allowed to grow up with the dreams of a little girl secure in her place in the world. That's not how my story went, but God always has a second plan. I heard someone say once in teaching over faith in God's provision that God is not surprised by our needs. He spoke about how God did not go into panic when Adam and Eve fell in the garden or when Jesus had 5,000 men and their families to feed. God didn't say, "Oh no, Gabriel! What am I going to do about this?" That's a humorous picture, but it's an accurate depiction of how we tend to picture God's hand in our lives. We attach the values of our own fears and inabilities to the hand of God, and as a result, our faith is weakened, we are overcome with fear, and we don't get the answers we so desperately need because we won't even ask for them let alone believe for them.

The story of Jonah taught me that God always has a plan B to carry out His will in my life—which isn't over. I struggled to hold enough faith to believe that my life could be much more than the grace to avoid ending up dead in a ditch somewhere, that there was hope.

The greatest hurdle I had to overcome was the intense feeling of disillusionment I was experiencing in regard to the church. I spent a year at a church where I struggled to trust what looked like a system and people who seemed mechanical in their interactions. I felt nauseous every time I walked through the doors, and I held tightly to my defiance of vulnerability in any church setting.

Growing up in the church I did under the pressure of so much guilt and shame and the effort of holding up underneath it all, I imagined its unleashing as being some ominous thing. It would bring the same catastrophic effects to those involved as they did to me, and people would be held accountable. I weighed that perceived justice against the pain it would cause and said nothing. When the disclosures were made and I was asked to confirm them, I did. No accountability or even an apology for the horror I grew up in followed. The leadership of the denomination worked to keep everything politically unmarred.

I continued doing all the things I had been doing, just going through the motions for years. My ability to distinguish that building from the one I had been molested in all those years before had vanished, and I felt nothing—I disconnected. Church was a machine, not a body. The level of disillusionment I experienced during those years was intense, and it only intensified as time went on. My heart hardened more as I tried to pull back out of a hole I hadn't realized I'd fallen into.

When we finally left the church, instead of feeling the relief I thought I'd feel walking away from where it all happened, everything intensified. The few weeks of panic attacks and nightmares that followed those disclosures were nothing compared to the panic, guilt, and shame I felt walking into the next three churches we tried. I was clearly the common denominator, but I couldn't shake how justified my fears and judgments seemed.

The nightmares about being raped in church and disregarded and being in constant danger and conflict with those in the church I grew up in only intensified my fears. One week, I walked into the church we had attended for the majority of that year after the singing had started. The lights were off except for the lighting on stage for worship. I froze. The usher asked how many, and I couldn't answer.

She asked that a few times, and I finally snapped out of it. That church was connected through several people in leadership to the leadership of the one we had left, and I often heard comments about how I was missed and needed back there as my pastor's right hand along with the looks of scorn and disapproval I got from others connected.

What I remembered was the irritation and frustration I saw in her eyes as I tried to work through what was happening in my heart, the panic I felt every week trying to sit through church with my parents; allowing them access to my children seemed so irrational. My pastor kept talking to me about not being bitter, about walking in forgiveness and restoration. I explained to her that I wasn't bitter. There was no admission of any wrongdoing, no remorse, no willingness to take any responsibility for our growing up. I heard from others in the church how my mom had told them what a handful we had been growing up, all that we had put her through. The abuse hadn't ended when we became adults; it just changed. I told her that I didn't want relationship or restoration, just rest.

Leaving her was heartbreaking because I loved and respected her so much and because I saw the disappointment and disapproval in her eyes so often when she looked at me. I spent a lot of time during that year mourning the loss I felt over that relationship.

Through friends, I was reminded of a church I'd known about but had never attended. I knew I couldn't sustain my spirit outside a church family, but there I was kicking myself for being stupid enough to even consider putting myself in a position to be hurt again. So there I was attending the fourth church in a year knowing in my spirit where we were supposed to be. It was the first time in years I wasn't nauseous as I sat down—no panic attacks or urges to react with hand-to-hand combat toward anyone within reach.

As I walked into that church and contemplated making commitments to it and the community there and beginning to serve again, I felt ready to bolt at any moment. I felt broken and worn with nothing to offer. But then I felt this crazy calling to allow God to use the destruction that I had survived through His grace to glorify His miraculous power to restore.

In John 9 is a story about a man who had been blind from birth. The disciples asked Jesus whether it was his sin or that of his parents that had caused his blindness. Jesus told them that it was neither, that the work of God would be made manifest in him.

And John 11 tells about the death of Lazarus. Mary was grieving the loss of her brother when Jesus arrived. She said she knew that He was the Messiah and that God would give Him anything He asked for, but Lazarus had been in the tomb for four days and stunk by that time. I stunk. My spirit was a wasteland, and I was rotting from the inside out. I knew the power of God, but I struggled to believe His power was still available to me. My spirit had been in the tomb for years, and instead of running to God, I had in my heart walked away, and I couldn't see how God could— would, really—deliver me from the tomb I found myself in.

Jesus told Mary that if she believed, she would see the glory of God. I needed the glory of God in my life, and I knew there was a call on my life to share that with others who had spent time in that tomb. The humanity behind the struggle is part of the testimony—we are imperfect, untidy, unruly, and stinky, but in God's eyes, we are lovely. He does not despise us; He loves us in whatever condition we are in. His eyes fill with the hope and joy set before Him.

I looked around, and the interactions I saw felt genuine. I felt my guard coming down, but that time, I wasn't afraid; I was more like curious. I didn't zone out or lose track of the message, the dissociative tendencies I had struggled with for so long. I left quickly but with a quiet knowing in my heart that God was doing something in me. I knew we had found our church home. I loved the vision and the excitement I felt in the people as the pastors shared their hearts with the community. I sat in the service remembering all the areas of ministry I had been involved in feeling so broken and wanting to scream, "Don't ask! I have nothing to offer!"

Small groups and an upcoming women's event were announced. When I was asked to join the children's ministry team, I began to pull back again concerned where they'd let me work if they really knew where I had come from and where I was then. I had a conversation with the pastor's wife in which I laid it all out. To my amazement, nothing changed. I broke through a wall at a two-day women's encounter where the presence of God was so strong, I had broken my cardinal rule within the first hour—I was crying my eyes out. I picked up all my stuff, walked to my car, and began loading the trunk. The whole way, I was thinking about why it was reasonable to leave. *I can't stay. I couldn't be vulnerable here to You with these people.* In my heart, I heard, *Then why did you come?* The answer was that I wanted a tender heart again. I wanted to be able to be sensitive to the Holy Spirit and walk in the calling I knew was on my life. I wanted my words to be seasoned with salt so I would always have an answer for my hope, an idea that seemed so unattainable at the time that I could hardly bear it. I went back inside and spent the entire day raw with vulnerability, crying before the Lord, and letting go all my frustrations and hurts in exchange for a peace I hadn't known.

As I submitted myself again to God under the ministry of these pastors, the Holy Spirit reminded me of all the things that had been planted in my heart over the years under divine protection as God ministered such spiritual wealth to me even in the place where I had experienced so much pain.

For the work that God speaks is alive and full of power making it active, operative, energizing, effective; it is sharper than any two-edged sword penetrating to the dividing line of the breath of life (soul) and the immortal spirit, and of joints and morrow [of the deepest parts of our nature] exposing and sifting and analyzing and judging the very thoughts and purposes of the heart. And not a creature exists that is concealed from his site that all things are open and exposed naked and defenseless to the eyes of him with whom we have to do. (Hebrews 4: 11 AMP)

CHAPTER 4

Coming Home

It isn't easy coming home like the Prodigal Son, who humbled himself and returned but wasn't sure if he'd be accepted. I'd spent years in the desert mourning what I'd lost as a child and the pain and hardship I had endured as a result. Timidly, like a child meeting someone for the first time, I tiptoed to the throne of God, and miraculously, I was home. Isaiah reads,

> Fear not, for you shall not be ashamed;
> neither be confounded and depressed, for
> you shall not be put to shame. For you shall
> forget the shame of your youth and you shall
> not seriously remember the reproach of your
> widowhood anymore. For your Maker is

your Husband—the Lord of Hosts is His name—and the Holy One of Israel is your Redeemer; the God of the whole earth He is called. For the Lord has called you like a woman forsaken, grieved in spirit and heart sore—even a wife wooed and won in youth, when she is later refused and scorned, says your God ... For though the mountain should depart or the hills be shaken or removed, yet my love and kindness shall not depart from you, nor shall My covenant of peace and completeness be removed, says the Lord, Who has compassion on you. (Isaiah 54:4–6, 10 AMP)

The sacrifice Jesus made for us when He died was so complex, so multifaceted; it encompasses every aspect of our lives. On the cross, He redeemed everything that was going to go wrong in anyone's life. He became sin for us so we could be the righteousness of God in Christ Jesus. He didn't just pay the price of our sin; He became it. He bore the the weight of our sin on His shoulders. Imagine the horror He felt as for the first time in eternity

He experienced the effects of the sin nature on His body and spirit, the shame that coursed through Him, and His Father turning from Him. He became every liar, thief, murderer, adulterer, drug addict, and even the worst of the worst so we could be redeemed.

Going back home felt like the walk of shame for me. In my early twenties, I began this journey with a question, *How can I ever get there?* All I felt was shame if I allowed myself to feel anything. I was carrying the entirety of everything I had experienced. My mantra was that I should have been louder, stronger, smarter, and more worthy of saving. *If I wasn't worth saving then, why now?* If I had been more attuned to the Spirit of God—I was raised in church after all—I would have known how to be all that I wasn't. That had made me vulnerable and weak, an easy target.

But God told me very clearly to stop asking why. I saw myself driving a car on a road that represented my life. He showed the question why to me as a huge building on that road, and it was impermeable. I saw my windshield and how it was there to protect me, how it allowed me to see what was coming and blocking the wind. Then I saw how small the rearview mirror was. God told me that if I continued to look behind me and ignore what was ahead, I would crash and it would be fatal. At times, I was tempted to stare into that rearview mirror, but God was faithful to keep me until I was ready and His timing was fulfilled.

He gave me scripture in those early years out of Hebrews 11, the Heroes' Hall of Fame as it is sometimes referred to. Hebrews 11:1 (AMP) reads, "Now faith is the assurance of the things we hope for, being the proof of things we do not see and the conviction of their reality [faith perceiving as real fact what is not revealed to the senses]." I didn't understand how God would do what I knew in my heart He was promising to do, but I had that tiny bit of faith that supernaturally implants in each one of us that He could give me the faith to believe. So on through the chapter, I read of all these great people of God, their incredible walks of faith before the term *walk of faith* was even a thing! Then in these verses, I read something I would need to hold onto for years.

All these people were still living by faith when they died. They did not receive the things promised; they only saw them and welcomed them from a distance, admitting that they were foreigners and strangers on earth. People who say such things show that they are looking for a country of their own. If they had been thinking of the country they had left, they would have had opportunity to return. Instead, they were longing for a better country—a heavenly one. Therefore God is not ashamed to be called their God, for he has prepared a city for them. (Hebrews 11:13–16 KJV)

God's timing is perfect, and I wasn't ready to face those years; I had not been strong enough physically or spiritually. It took fifteen years under a phenomenal pastor and the anointing she stood in for me before I came to the place where I could begin to heal. During those years, my walk with the Lord became stronger. I learned how to stand in faith for the day-to-day things such as getting out of bed in the morning and believing I'd still be around to do the same thing the next day. I learned how to pray, to intercede, and to see the needs of others. I practiced seeing God as so much bigger than my day-to-day hurdles.

But He didn't stop there. Psalm 103 (AMP) reads, "Bless the Lord oh my **soul**," [the mind, will and emotions] "and all that is [deepest] within me, bless His holy name … and forget not **all** of His benefits. [He] forgives every one of all your iniquities … Redeems your life from the pit and corruption."

Iniquity is defined as gross injustice, a wicked act or thing. To redeem is to buy back, to free from what distresses or harms. There is nothing we have walked through willingly or unwillingly that has not been paid for on our behalf. Some of the iniquity in my life has been completely outside my ability to control or change. Some of it I walked through because I couldn't see another way out, and some I walked through because I was mad about it and didn't want another way out. God saw through all of it and paid for it with His Son. I was chained in sin, but God gave Jesus as ransom for me so I could go free. I don't ever want to disregard that sacrifice by walking back in to the bondage and away from the freedom that was paid for so dearly.

God heals all our diseases. According to the CDC, about 600,000 people die of heart disease in the US every year, and our spiritual hearts are not immune to disease. In the natural world, as destructive things go into our bodies, our hearts' ability to carry life through us is impaired as our veins and arteries begin to become blocked. Without intervention, our hearts finally give up and our bodies are cut off from their life-giving source. Our spiritual hearts are similar. As we go through life, destructive things happen. We carry some hurt here and some shame there all the while inhibiting our spiritual hearts' ability to carry life to our spirits. I got so plugged up with years of hurt and disappointment that my spiritual heartbeat was so faint that I wasn't even sure it was there. The blood of Jesus is our source of life. Bless the Lord, oh my soul. He made provision for my broken heart, making way for the life of God to pulse through me again!

God beautifies, dignifies, and crowns us with loving-kindness and tender mercies. The brassy quality I found in my walk with the Lord was ugly and pitiful, and it made walking in love so difficult. Just as Jonah waited for the city of Nineveh to be burned to the ground, I looked for the wrath of God to fall on some people. I wasn't looking for loving-kindness and tender mercies in their lives. I wasn't reaping the benefits of those things in my life either. It was the place between my realization of what my life had been, my willingness to acknowledge the pain it had caused, and God intervening to help me see the grace that had been on me all along. It was a process of healing during which I did not appear to possess any of the qualities above. As God was purging the destruction that happened to me, He was faithful to purge the destruction that happened in me.

God satisfies our mouths—our necessities and desires—with good so that our youth, renewed, is like the eagle's—strong, overcoming, and soaring!

We've been forgiven, redeemed, healed, and restored. We're filled with loving-kindness and tender mercies. Our hearts have been changed. Proverbs 4:23 (AMP) tells us, "Keep and guard your heart with all vigilance and above all that you guard, for out of it flow the springs of life." Proverbs 4:20–22 (AMP) reads "My son, attend to my words; consent and submit to my sayings. Let them not depart from your sight; keep them in the **center of your**

heart. For they are life to those who find them, healing and health to all their flesh." We can maintain the newness of our hearts by giving His Word first place in our lives and keeping it at the center of our hearts. Jesus became sin so we could be in right standing with God.

Therefore, since we are surrounded by so great a cloud of witnesses [who by faith have testified to the truth of God's absolute faithfulness], stripping off every unnecessary weight and the sin which so easily and cleverly entangles us, let us run with endurance and active persistence the race that is set before us, [looking away from all that will distract us and] focusing our eyes on Jesus, who is the Author and Perfecter of faith [the first incentive for our belief and the One who brings our faith to maturity], who for the joy [of accomplishing the goal] set before Him endured the cross, disregarding the shame, and sat down at the right hand of the throne of God [revealing His deity, His authority, and the completion of His work]. (Hebrews 11:1–2 AMP)

I don't know all that God has in store for my life, what His plan B might look like, but I'm excited in a way I've never been before. My healing process hasn't been instantaneous, but my willingness hasn't been either. Two decades of grief take some time to unearth when it's been buried as far down as I buried it.

At times, I still struggle with the same thought patterns I have for so many years, but I also have the tools to stay present, and my relationship with the Lord is being restored more everyday as I continue my journey in learning to trust Him, seeing His body as an extension of Him instead of the mechanical joke it had become for me. It's been an amazing journey of the grace and mercy of God on my life every day, and it's not over yet!

The Song of My Heart:

"Ancient Ruin" 2002

The world was the hammer that drove the nails in

Our tears were the nails that pierced His skin

His blood was the rain that fell that day

Proving love the only way

To wash again a heart like mine

Who am I to call on the Divine?

I've spent some time in Ancient Ruin

Save me, save me! My heart cried out

Seemed muffled by my fear and doubt

Could love wash even this away?

Could hope show me a fresher day?

How do I break free from Ancient Ruin?

My heart was stale, old, and gray

But it was for me a debt was paid

The sun must shine, and dark must leave

If to Jesus I will cleave

I lift mine eyes—whence comes my help?

I need to cry, I look to the skies

Darkness, Shame, Broken Dreams

Take flight, I shout, away from me

I trust in the Lord, Purge me, God

Make me clean, Take the doubt

I call on You with all my might

Take me Lord, make me right

Again.

Come, come! His heart cries out

Wounds and bruises bleed proof of redemption

My peace was wrought upon His shoulders

The stripes He bore so deafeningly shout:

"I'm at the right hand, and with you yet

Making intercession, you I cannot forget

Your tears were the nails that pierced My skin

My blood is the rain that cleanses all sin

I wait as the groom longs for His bride

Come to My throne, look at My side

The pain you feel was the spear that marked

Your victory over pain, and bondage to the dark"

Save me, save me! My heart cried out

So He's taken all the fear and doubt

And love has washed my sins away

In hope I breathe a fresher day

He's broken off the chains

Of Ancient Ruin

THE
BEGINNING